Body Language explained by an Ex-CIA Agent

By

MARK GRANT

Table of Contents

Introduction

I have been studying body language for quite some time and the virtues of these brilliant techniques are unfathomable. Reading body language is all about knowing what is in the mind of the other person without even talking to them. It may seem similar to mind reading, but all you are doing is reading the cues left by a person's body to analyze what they could possibly be thinking.

I have always been interested in body language, mostly because of the way it is represented in popular culture. Apparently, you have to be some sort of genius in order to read body language. I always thought it was impossible to read body language like that, and it was all a sham.

Well, I was certainly wrong. It is all true. You will be able to predict almost every single thought that going in a person's mind just by reading their body language. It's not easy, that's for sure. You need to have an eagle eye and be very smart. But it is definitely possible.

I know that it's possible because of my interactions with an ex-CIA agent, whose name I cannot disclose. It was merely by luck that I found him and I must say, interacting with him has been a fun ride. Oh, the things he has told me!

He is the one who taught me how to read body language. According to him, most human beings don't know how to hide the way the body naturally reacts when they are feeling certain emotions. For someone trying to read your body, it makes their job easier.

I wrote this book so you can all drink from the infinite pool of knowledge that my dear friend gave to me. I hope this is book will be helpful, and will be enough information to satisfy your thirst for knowledge.

Chapter 1: Body Language of a CIA Agent

The first step in decoding body language is to learn the ideal type of body language. So, let's go ahead and learn what the body language of a CIA agent looks like.

In my conversations with my friend, I was told that all CIA agents are taught to control their body movements to ensure that they do not end up giving their thoughts away. This is important when working in the field, because CIA agents aren't the only people who can read body language—enemy soldiers are trained just as thoroughly, and are able to read agent body language.

It is important to control your body, because your body can betray your thoughts. Even if you don't intentionally move, your body reacts to your emotions. For instance, if you are nervous, you might start shaking your leg. There are many different kinds of reactions that your body experiences, and all of them are windows to what you are thinking. A trained individual will be able to know what you're thinking easily while observing you.

So, let's start with the various ways in which you can control your body's reactions.

Emotions

Most people tend to express their emotions through their face. Of course, there are other ways to express emotion, but facial expressions are the easiest to read and the typical bodily response to emotions. They are extremely obvious, and are therefore the most accurate way to get a read on someone.

It is important to get a grip on the way you show emotions. For example—crying is a way we try to convey sadness. This is extremely obvious, but at the same time, it is important to control your urge to cry. I am one of those people who starts bawling their eyes out at the smallest thing. My CIA friend told me that I am not the only one. People might seem tough, but most people tend to cry very easily. If you ever feel the urge cry, the best thing to do is to bite your lips. The pain from this should stop you from crying.

Holding a blank face is another important way to hide your emotions. The face is a dead giveaway for your thoughts. So, make sure you have a blank face at all times. Keeping a blank face is not that easy. If you try too hard it seems pretty obvious.

In order to ensure that you never give anything away with your facial expressions, my CIA friend gave me an ingenious tip: Whenever you have to hide your true feelings, always imagine a puppy getting strangled in front of you. I know it sounds horrid, but it's the best way. This will remind you to change your expression to a blank face. After a certain point, it will become more instinctual for your face to maintain a neutral expression.

Chapter 2: How to Analyze People

We finally arrive at the best part of the book. In this section, I'll brief you on the various tricks that can be used to read people. Reading people is not an easy job, and there are times you might get frustrated because of the how hard it is. The main goal for this book is to remind you to practice. When I asked my CIA friend how he mastered the art of reading people, he told me that the best way to master reading someone is to constantly keep doing it. Like any skill, it takes continuous practice to make it instinctual.

In simple terms, what my friend was trying to say is, if you continuously read those around you, then reading people becomes second nature to you. You'll always read people, no matter who you are talking to. This way, you will be able to pick up cues within the conversation you wouldn't have otherwise understood: you can spot lies, understand people better, improving your overall communication skills.

It's especially important to read the people that you know well. If you know someone personally, it's easier to read them. You might have been reading those close to you without even knowing it. Many people know exactly when their partners are tired or want to go out; this is because your subconscious is always trying to read the body language of those that are around you. All you have to do now is be consciously aware of this fact, and soon you'll be able to read complete strangers as well.

Here are a few of the best methods for reading people:

Posture

The body is the best way to read someone. You can know everything about a person, depending on the way they handle their body. People are easily attracted to others depending on the way they carry themselves. This is because your subconscious reads into the way someone walks or talks, and picks upon desirable traits.

The body is a way to nonverbally communicate with other people; what you think tends to show up subconsciously in your actions. As we discussed earlier, you might shake your leg when you're nervous, or you could bite or purse your lips if you're uncomfortable in a particular setting.

The way you hold yourself will either attract people or it can lead to a bad impression. Our brain is always reading others even if we are not. You might have noticed how people are attracted to people who are very confident. That's because those people leave a long-lasting impression on your subconscious. You might not realize it, but your subconscious is flooding you with information at all times.

This can also help you study yourself. Try to concentrate on your own thoughts while you are standing or sitting, trying to listen to your own subconscious. The gut feelings or instincts that you have are all triggered by your subconscious telling you something. If walking in a certain way makes you feel really confident and good about yourself, then try to mimic that in real life.

You can differentiate between the different ways people talk as well. When some people talk, it seems as if they are more caring or kind. Your voice is a way through which people can try to read you. You can always relate an adjective to someone's voice. If someone has a deep and heavy voice, then your automatic response is to assume that they are strong. The reason behind this is your subconscious reading into their body language. They might not actually be strong but that's the assumption you make.

Eyes

Eye contact is something that will always give you reliable results. Your eyes are a perfect representation of your feelings. Your eyes can convey to another person what you are feeling. You are never aware of the state of your eyes. Your eyes contract or expand to show certain feelings. Unfortunately, these are things are hardly noticeable. It's very difficult to figure out eye-related reactions, simply because the eyes are smaller compared to the rest of your face and you need to get really close to a person to be able to read their eyes. But never fear, your subconscious helps you here too.

It is a universal phenomenon that there are certain chemical reactions that we experience, which are represented in our eyes. Common emotions (such as affection, anger, etc.), are always shown through the eyes. It is impossible to hide such reactions. This is why it's easier for your subconscious to decipher eye-related reactions. Your brain knows exactly what the contraction or expansion of the eyes means. Hence, it can easily decipher the thoughts of another person through their eyes. The only problem is that you won't be able to understand such things yourself. The only way to understand emotions through the movements of the eye is to listen to your instincts.

The only thing you have to do is look the other person in the eye. That's your only job. You don't have to think anything letting your brain do all the work. All you have to do is try to listen to your gut and go with your instincts.

It's also possible to read eye-related reactions yourself, but it takes a lot of time and practice. You have to notice minute details. This is not easy, and you need to keep practicing. It's obviously not everyone's cup of tea. Therefore, it is suggested that you let your instincts take over rather than try to decipher eye-related reactions yourself.

The only reason you might want to do this is because it can be difficult to read your instincts, or gut. It's not like you have to actually look inside yourself for answers; it is something that comes naturally. If you feel like you can't read your own instincts, then you can definitely try to read someone through their eyes. It is difficult, but there is a pretty good chance that you will be able to do it.

Facial Expressions

The face is said to be one of the most common ways to read body language, but it is also the most unreliable. This is because almost everyone is an expert at hiding their emotions—at least to an extent. So, the expression you might see on someone's face could very well be fake. It is also possible to alter our expressions according to our need. This is something that you cannot do with the rest of your body. Your body language replicates the emotions that you are feeling in such ways that even you are not aware of it.

The face is also the easiest to read. There are many emotions for which there are generally understood reactions: anger is pretty easy to identify it through your facial expressions.

You have to be very careful while reading someone's face. It is the easiest way to read someone, but also the most unreliable. You simply have to understand when someone is being fake and when someone is not.

If you continuously study someone, you can be an expert at understanding them. You will know when they are being genuine and when they are not. It is better to avoid reading someone through their facial responses unless you have plenty of experience with, or know them personally; it is easier to differentiate between a genuine and a fake expression if you know someone very well. This is why partners find it difficult to hide things from each other.

Chapter 3: Reading Minds with Nonverbal Communication

Nonverbal communication is different from reading people. When you are trying to read people, all you do is look at their body language and try to learn what they are feeling. You won't ever get exact results. You can know that a person is scared, but you won't know why that person is scared.

Nonverbal communication, on the other hand, happens when your subconscious reads another person's body language, and reacts in a similar way, so the other person's subconscious can read your body language. This is an extension of the previous idea, only the communication becomes a two-way street, even if you don't realize it.

You may have been nonverbally communicating with people without even knowing it. A brilliant example of nonverbal communication is twins. Take, for example, how twins sometimes seem to know what is going on in each other's minds without talking.

Now comes the difficult part—how can you read the other person's mind with nonverbal communication? To do this, you need be in sync with your subconscious. Nonverbal communication comes naturally for humans. We communicate nonverbally without even knowing it. All you have to do in this scenario is to recognize when you are communicating nonverbally with someone.

Meditation helps a lot. If you practice a lot and are aware of the people around you, you'll instantly know when your mind is trying to read someone.

If you notice someone pulling closer to you, you might not pay attention to that, but your subconscious does. If you are not in sync with your subconscious you might not even notice that the other person was pulling closer to you, due to attraction.

Conclusion

I wrote this book so I could help people who wanted to know more about body language: reading and understanding it. I have been trying to read body language for quite some time and have made some brilliant progress, but at the same time, it has been a difficult journey.

What I have learned is that reading people is all about practice. For instance, the longer you do it, the more obvious it becomes when someone blinks too much when they are talking to you, which is a sign of nervousness.

Reading body language is a social advantage. It will help you to be a better person and you will be able to react more emotionally to situations. You can use it for various purposes, but try not to depend on it too much. It can be harmful if you start reading too much into something and jump to conclusions.

Another important point is that reading people is not really an exact science. Sometimes people react in different ways due to a variety of variables that are not related to their emotions at all. So, it's important to not rely too much on reading someone's body language unless you are a professional CIA agent who has had years of training.

I hope that this book turned out to be useful and that you were able to learn something from it.

Navy Seals

Self-Discipline

*Training and Self-Discipline to Become Tough
Like A Navy SEAL*

Introduction

You might have heard about Navy SEALs, but do you know everything about what they do? A quick background will help you get a better understanding.

Navy SEALS are one of the most elite group of fighters in the world, but there is so much more to being a SEAL than fighting. They do operate in a world that's far different from our own, but their training can prove to be a useful weapon in your arsenal for achieving success.

Quick background

In the year 1962, under the orders of President Kennedy, the United States Navy had established a special sea, air, and land team known as Navy SEALS. The Navy SEALS are considered to be an elite group of specialists who are trained to engage in unconventional combat. High-impact missions that require stealth—which cannot be carried out by large forces like tanks and submarines—are carried out by the SEALs. For all the operations that either start or end in water bodies like swamps, oceans, coastlines, and so on, the go-to team of specialists for Navy, Air Force, and even Army Special Forces would be the SEALs. Though the Navy SEALs belong to the naval unit of United States, they are trained to engage in missions on all types of terrains and extreme climatic conditions as well.

This book contains proven steps and strategies on how to train yourself mentally, physically, and emotionally like a Navy SEAL to achieve your goals. Well, it is likely that you won't be on par with the well-trained SEALs but you can definitely make use of their principles in your day-to-day life.

Chapter One: Training Regimen of Navy Seals

Mind Over Matter

The human body is made up of many different organs, but the brain is considered to be the most powerful of all. You wouldn't be able to perform even the simplest of functions—like moving your muscles—if your brain wasn't functioning. You might have heard stories of heroism performed by men on battlefields that saved not just their lives but also of those around them. They wouldn't have been able to do so if they weren't mentally strong. Navy SEALs are trained in such a manner that their brain can override their physical pain and push them to function in a manner that would usually seem impossible. Mental preparation is the key to unlocking your true potential.

The brain is a muscle, and you will be able to train it by engaging in some mental exercises. You can do these mental exercises any time and place. You can exercise your mind to unlock your potential by engaging your mind in the following exercises.

Battle-proofing will help you to condition your mind to react in hostile situations and emergencies, by developing mental strength for managing a crisis. This can be done by visualizing intense fights. When you start battle-proofing your brain, it will start believing that you have experienced all that you have imagined. Whenever a similar situation comes up, you will be able to take quick action.

You will need to create your own "triggers." A trigger is something that can help you ignite the qualities that are necessary for not just your survival but for your personal growth as well. Your trigger could be a memory, a phrase, or an experience that can move your mind and soul towards achieving your goals.

You should train your mind to get out of situations that would stress you out unnecessarily and this will help you to gain control over a situation.

Navy SEALs are trained not to act on the first impulse that pops into their mind, but to consider all the possible ways of acting in a critical situation. You will be able to do this only when you can reign in your thoughts and control your mind.

When you are truly aware of your insecurities and true motivations, you will be able to avoid making the same mistakes again and can move forward. Understanding the purpose behind your job, whether you are a Navy SEAL or not, will help you excel. Learn to make yourself as happy as you can be in any given situation and don't do anything halfheartedly.

Have faith in yourself, surround yourself with positive company, always focus on the present, and don't live in your past or future. Lastly, learn to control your breathing. Navy SEALs are tough men, not just because of their bodies but because of their minds as well.

Various Stages of Training

Warfare preparatory school

The training curriculum for becoming a Navy SEAL starts at the Naval Special Warfare Preparatory School referred to as NSW Prep, in Great Lakes, Illinois, and lasts for 8 weeks. The aim of NSW Prep is to prepare the SEAL candidates to endure the grueling physical trials of BUD/S. NSW Prep ends with a PST that you must pass if you want to become a SEAL. It begins with a Physical Screening Test and ends with a grueling PST that includes a 1,000 yard swim to be completed in or under 20 minutes, 60 curl-ups in 2 minutes, 70 push-ups in 2 minutes, 10 pull-ups in 2 minutes, and a four mile run with shoes and pants that needs to be completed within 31 minutes.

BUD/S Training – 3 phases

BUD/S stands for Basic Underwater Demolition/SEAL Training, and this helps to develop the physical and mental strength of the candidates who want to become Navy SEALs. BUD/S lasts for 7 months and has different phases that test the physical, emotional, mental strength, and also leadership skills of the candidates. BUD/S has a three-week orientation, followed by the three phases mentioned below.

Indoctrination:

This lasts for three weeks, and introduces the candidates to the BUD/S lifestyle at Coronado: the Naval Special Warfare Center. The INDOC is designed to help prepare the candidates for the training they have to undergo in the three phases.

Phase 1: The first phase lasts for seven weeks and it assesses the SEAL candidates in different areas of physical conditioning: proficiency in water, teamwork skills, and mental strength. Physical conditioning includes swimming, running, and calisthenics, and the course grows harder every week. The first two weeks of this training prepares them for the third week, also referred to as "hell week". The candidate has to take part in five and a half days of strenuous training with maybe 4 hours of sleep for the entire week, and the training can exceed 20 hours a day. After the "hell week," the remaining 4 weeks are spent learning different methods of creating hydrographic charts and conducting various hydrographic surveys.

Phase 2: This lasts for 7 weeks and is the diving phase, aimed at training and developing the SEAL candidates' skills as combat swimmers. The physical training becomes more intensive and focuses on combat scuba. It focuses on open as well as closed circuit scuba. Basic medical training and dive medicine skills training is given. This phase helps make sure that the applicants are capable of making use of swimming and diving techniques as transportation from their basic launch points. If a candidate wants to complete the second phase, they would have to showcase an extreme level of comfort and ability to perform in stressful and tough circumstances.

Phase 3: This lasts for 7 weeks and trains the candidates in land warfare like the usage of basic weapons, land navigation, demolitions, patrolling, rappelling, and small unit tactics. There is a lot of classroom work that teaches them to read maps, use compass, and to collect and process information for completing their mission. These skills allow the candidates to become more comfortable while out in the field.

For the last three and a half weeks of the training, the class is taken offshore to San Clemente Island. Here they get to practice all the skills that they have acquired in the third phase. The training and work becomes more intensive in order to mirror the work they get in field. This is the most intensive part of training, because the training goes on for all seven days of the week with minimal sleep, while handling dangerous explosives and ammunition. Also, the punishments for mistakes at this stage of training are extremely harsh.

Parachute Jump School:

After the completion of BUD/S the SEAL candidates proceed to San Diego, California to learn static and free fall training at Tactical Air Operations. This is a 3-week program that is conducted by highly trained and qualified instructors and it is designed to help transform the SEAL candidates into competent free fall jumpers within a short duration of time. At the end of the training they should be able to complete night descents in all their combat equipment from an altitude of at least 9500 feet.

Graduation

The SEALs training concludes with the BUD/S class graduation, where the candidates who managed to survive the grueling training stand proud in their Navy uniform and receive the pins with the Trident insignia, the symbol of becoming an official Navy SEAL. The achievements of the new SEAL recruits are recognized in the presence of various senior SEAL leaders, Senior advisors of Naval Special Warfare groups, Naval Commanding Officers, other SEAL teams, and family members.

Post-graduation training

The SEAL training doesn't end with becoming a part of the SEALs. Even after graduation, they continue to be put through extensive training before they are sent out into the field on missions. The BUD/S was just a qualifying training program and it is only after continuous training will they be qualified as SEALs officially.

Once the recruits have been assigned to a particular SEAL Team, then their troop training begins. This is pre-deployment training, it can last from 12-18 months, and is divided into three phases that include: individuality specialty training, unit level training, and task group level training.

The training that they go through is extremely tough and testing on the body, mind, and spirit. Going through it might not be possible for all of us, but we can definitely implement a few of their practices in our daily life for becoming more successful.

What is Navy SEAL Self-Discipline and Why Should you learn from them?

The reason for this is simply, training like a Navy SEAL will make you more confident in yourself. When you are mentally, physically, and emotionally strong, you will never feel incapable of achieving something that you want. You needn't be a Navy SEAL in order to win, you just need to adopt a few of their principles.

Physical fitness

Being physically fit and in shape does go a long way when it comes to boosting your self-confidence. This might sound vain, or even superficial, but it's the truth. Training the way that SEALs do will definitely help you achieve great physical strength and fitness.

Mental Toughness

Most of the battles that we face in our life are mental or emotional. The SEALs are considered to be amongst the world's physically superior specimens, but their mental conditioning is just as important as their physical superiority. Most of the time, it's mental trauma that cripples them. Only those who are mentally and emotionally fit can survive being a SEAL. This will also make you a confident person.

Situational Awareness

Being aware of yourself and the situation you are in can help a great deal when you are on the path towards achieving your goals. You shouldn't have any illusions about who you are and what you are doing. Always be sensitive to your surroundings and this will help you figure out exits and different strategies for getting yourself where you want to be.

Quick Action

Being able to take quick action in a situation of crisis is extremely important for the SEALs. In the situations they usually find themselves in, even a small mistake or delay can prove to be life threatening—not just for themselves, but for those around them as well. You can condition your mind to act in a certain manner in a specific situation and when the time comes, your mind will automatically do what it has been programmed to do instead of wasting precious time figuring out a course of action.

Chapter Two: How To Develop Self Discipline the SEAL Way: Part I

Through Improving Physical Fitness

Due to the extremely demanding situations they have to face, Navy SEALs always have to stay in their finest physical shape if they want to carry out their missions successfully. Navy SEALs need to be in good cardiovascular shape, nimble, strong, and quick. Cardio and calisthenics are the most important aspects of their physical fitness programs.

Cardio

Navy SEALs usually have to disembark really far from shores in order to approach the enemy territory as stealthily as possible. At times they need to swim great distances with their weapons and gear on. Well, if you swim, you might realize that swimming in a pool for 10 laps can drain you completely, but if you have to swim with all the added weight of your weapons, that's really tough. You needn't swim 1 kilometer in the open sea or run 1.5 miles under 11 minutes while wearing your army boots, but doing cardio regularly will help you to stay in great shape. Cardio helps to increase your heart rate and improves the delivery of oxygen to the various muscles in the body to burn out all the fat. The most practical way of doing cardio is running. You just need a pair of good running shoes and you are set. The only limitation that you will have to overcome is your mind. Swimming, cycling, and even jogging are good forms of cardio.

Calisthenics

Bodyweight exercises are an extremely important part of fitness regimes, and calisthenics helps you to stay in shape without building any excess muscle. When it comes to combat, functional strength is the most important factor that you should take into consideration. Lifting strength and functional strength are extremely different. For example, scaling a wall requires functional strength and not lifting strength—a gymnast would be able to scale a wall easily when compared to a bodybuilder who can pull down 400 pounds! Grip push-ups, pull-ups, bodyweight back extensions, squats, lunges, jumping squats, sit-ups, crunches, planks, burpees, trunk twists, and so on are good calisthenics exercises. You can start out by working three times a week and increase it to four to five times a week. Make sure that you are working out all the muscle groups and not overdoing it.

Yoga

Yoga is extremely good for developing mental and physical strength. Your mind will become more alert and you will feel yourself getting stronger spiritually as well. There are different yoga poses that you can do depending upon the part of the body that you want to work on. Breathing exercises will help you to calm your mind, and ensure the optimum supply of oxygen to various parts of your body for their better functioning. *Anulom vilom, kapalbhati and Bhrastrika pranayama* will help you regulate your breathing. Yoga poses like tree pose, cobra pose, triangle pose, shoulder stand pose, plough pose, bow pose, fish pose, forward bend, downward dog, and child's pose will help in developing core strength.

Running

Running is an important part of Navy SEAL training, and you will need to concentrate on form and effort to improve your running potential. If you want to build your stamina, then long slow distance would be the most ideal style to start with. Agility is extremely important for SEALs because they need to traverse great distances on foot and run around a lot while carrying all their ammunition and gear. Running at a consistent, moderate pace for long distance will improve your stamina greatly. Continuous high intensity running is tough, but it will help you achieve and maintain a great speed for a longer duration of time. You can also adopt high intensity exercises combined with short intervals between them, like cross fit.

Through Improving Nutrition

Aside from performing all the rigorous activities and exercises that the SEALs have to, they also need to have nutritious food daily. When it comes to physical health as well as fitness, nutrition plays a very important role. You might have seen people who regularly and religiously work out at the gym and still look like the Michelin Man. This is because of their poor diet that's full of sugar and fats.

Diet plan for the whole day

Navy SEALs have a very demanding job and for them, having nutritional meals is very important to keep performing well. Navy SEALs follow NOFFS (Navy Operational Fitness and Fueling Series) for maintaining optimal nutrition. The NOFFS limits the consumption of processed foods and encourages the consumption of whole foods that are good for the body. High carbohydrate and protein consumption along with fiber is extremely important for SEALs, for maintaining their strength and stamina.

For good metabolism, SEALs eat small and frequent meals. They eat about 4 to 6 meals every day with a gap of at least two hours between each meal. This prevents binge eating and helps burn calories as well. This is a good way of eating, not just for the SEALs, but for everyone in general.

Consuming carbohydrates the size of your fist, proteins the size of your palm, dietary fats the size of tip of your thumb would be sufficient for a normal person.

A Navy SEAL would have his first meal before working out at 6:00 a.m., and it would include something that has a little fat content to keep them going, like an omelet made of egg whites and 2 slices of wheat toast. Eat as many grains as possible, but avoid white bread and pasta.

The second meal would be at 9:00 a.m. after working out and consumption of carbs is permitted now. This will help in the transportation of insulin throughout your body after the workout. 2 bananas with a glass of milk with reduced fat content, or oatmeal with raisins and skim milk is a good option as well. You can always add a fruit if you are hungry.

The third meal would be around 12:00 p.m., and this would be your lunch. Avoid oily and fried items as well as the stuff that you find in the vending machines. You can consider having a whole wheat wrap or sandwich with turkey in it and as many vegetables as you like except those that are high in carbs. A few baked potato chips would be good, and broccoli to maintain your fiber intake. Also, you can have a fruit or some yogurt for desert.

At 3:00 p.m. you can have your fourth meal that can consists of a can of tuna or some egg whites on a whole wheat bagel, or a slice of bread. Something light to keep your energy levels up and your hunger in check would be a good idea. Low fat yogurt and vegetables would be good too.

The fifth meal should be consumed around 5:00 p.m. and you can include something really light, because you would consume your dinner in a few hours. Have a small salad or a snack like wheat crackers to nibble on. A glass of fruit juice, protein shake, or even coconut water would make you feel energized. But avoid fat at all cost; you wouldn't want to regain all the fat that you burnt while working out.

The sixth meal for the day is dinner; have it at around 6:30 p.m. Include multigrain pasta or anything else that gives you some carbs and proteins, a little bit of bread, and some protein in the form of chicken or turkey breast, fish, or a really lean stake. Add in as many vegetables as you want and some greens to make a complete and healthy meal. Give yourself at least two to three hours before heading to bed so that your stomach can digest all that you have consumed.

Healthy Eating – Quick Tips

Here are some tips that you can keep in mind if you want to eat healthy every day, just like Navy SEALs –

- You can consume 5 to 6 meals every day that are spaced out with an interval of at least three hours between each meal. Consume small meals and don't binge.
- Don't skip your meals and make sure your diet is rich in protein, some complex carbs, and a little bit of fat as well, but not processed sugar. Eat till you feel full, but don't stuff yourself.
- Remember to exercise every day; don't skip this step. You needn't undergo the rigorous physical regimen followed by SEALs, but do exercise.
- Drink lots of water and keep yourself hydrated throughout the day. Drink some water before every meal and also after every meal. Keep a few healthy snacks on hand whenever hunger and cravings creep in.

- You should always chew your food well and don't swallow it without chewing. Don't starve yourself; eat regularly if you are having small meals.

Chapter Three: How To Develop Self Discipline the SEAL Way – Part II

Through Overcoming Fear

Fear can be crippling. If you overcome your fear you will be able to think clearly and you will be able to tackle the problem at hand in a better manner. But if you let your fear get a hold of you, then the outcome won't be positive. SEALs are trained in such a manner that their brains wouldn't let fear creep in. If you can also train your mind in a similar manner you will be able to discipline yourself and focus on your goals.

Habituation

The reason why SEALs are fearless when compared to other human beings is because of their training, and a psychological technique that is referred to as habituation. This is the process of exposing a person to things or situations that he or she is scared of, repeatedly. Repeated exposure will help the person to overcome their fears, because they start getting used to them and will be immune to it. This is a case of mind over matter. One of the primary weapons of the modern army are the minds of people who comprise it. For becoming a successful Navy SEAL you not only need to be physically fit but also mentally strong.

Setting Goals

Setting short-term and very specific goals will help you perform better. Set small goals that you know you will be able to accomplish with a little extra effort. When you complete or achieve a goal, it will fill you with a sense of accomplishment that will help you in not only performing better, but it will also improve your confidence and boot your morale. According to studies conducted by neuroscientists, the trainees who set short-term goals managed to have a higher rate of success than those who didn't. This technique can be used by anyone, not just the SEALs. Don't bother yourself with what might happen after you have completed the task. Instead, simply focus on the task at hand.

Visualization

This is a technique that is frequently used by sportsmen and even musicians when they want to improve their skills. Whenever they take a break, they visualize themselves as either performing or playing a piece of music perfectly, or swinging their bat really well. Practicing mental visualizations is as important as performing the task itself. During the training sessions, the SEALs have to don their scuba gear and perform emergency drills while underwater. All the while they might keep getting harassed by their instructor who would make the drill tougher by cutting off their oxygen supply or tying up the scuba pipes. In such a situation, they need to keep their calm and practice visualization, because this helps the brain to automatically switch to the mode where it does everything for achieving the goal on hand without much trouble. This is an incredible motivational technique that will definitely help in performing better. Your mind will want to experience the joy it experiences when you visualized the completion of the task, and this will push you to achieve the goal that was set.

Positive Self Talk

Did you know that you talk to yourself at a rate of anywhere between 800 to 1,600 words per minute? That's a lot, isn't it? Imagine if you engage in a negative conversation with yourself for 5 minutes, you will have said around 4,000 negative words to yourself. Well, that doesn't sound fair to you. Navy SEALs are taught simple techniques of self-hypnotism that help them overcome all of the negative thoughts, and instead helps them to focus their energy on positive thoughts and actions. This would act as a motivational factor and help them to move along when the going gets tough.

Through Developing Situational Awareness

Situational awareness is of great importance, especially for the Navy SEALs because they are often in such risky situations where one wrong move might prove to be fatal for themselves and all those around them. You can also improve your self-discipline by working on your situational awareness by doing the following.

Arousal Control

Being able to control your state of mind is a very important factor for the Navy SEALs. There are different knee-jerk reactions that are hardwired into our system and fine-tuning them can be quite difficult. For instance, sweaty palms and shaky hands are common symptoms of being scared or nervous. These are natural bodily reactions that are designed for helping you stay out of trouble. This is something that cannot be controlled, and is caused by strong hormones, like adrenaline and cortisol. Controlling the secretion of these hormones is also hard when you are stressed or scared. Navy SEALs are required to perform in extremely demanding circumstances and it is extremely important for them to control these knee-jerk reactions. Practicing deep breathing helps to control your reactions and clear your mind.

Waiting Patiently

Patience might not come easily, but it is a very important trait if you are a SEAL. You will need to be patient and you shouldn't rush anything without thinking things through. Your first thought or impulse might not always be right. There might be alternative ways of doing a single task; go through the possible list very patiently without rushing. This will help you in making the best decision. Impatience will just push you to make rash decisions that could harm you and all those around you. Learn to be patient and you can start to discipline your mind.

Controlling Breathing

Taking deep breaths is also a very effective relaxation technique and it also helps you to think clearly so that you don't make a hurried decision that can be potentially damaging. Whenever you feel that you are panicking, take a few deep breaths and close your eyes. This will help you to calm your mind so that you can think clearly once again without the veil of panic clouding your vision. A Navy SEAL needs to learn to think clearly even in situations of distress, and this skill will definitely come in handy.

Close Observation

Observational skills are very important, and developing them is no easy task. Whether you are a civilian or not, it takes a long time to develop these skills. For SEALs it is extremely important to develop their observational skills because it would help them in their survival! It becomes really difficult to develop this skill when you are a civilian, but it can be done by playing a simple game. The awareness game is something that will help you to develop your observational skills easily. Whenever you are outside, notice little things about those around you and make a mental note of what you observe. When you go home, recollect what you observed and compare the same with what others observed. In a life-threatening situation, like when you are stuck in fire, noticing and remembering a fire exit will definitely come in handy.

Self-discipline is important in every aspect of life, regardless of whether or not you are a Navy SEAL. It helps to control your impulses and to achieve the goals that you have set for yourself by taking the right course of action. When your mind is disciplined, there is nothing you cannot achieve.

Conclusion

I hope it was able to help you to understand the qualities that make Navy SEALs tough, and that you can also start training like them: physically, mentally, emotionally, and **also** nutritionally to become more confident. You might not become as tough as an actual Navy SEAL, but you can definitely achieve your goals by making use of the same principles.

The next step is to apply whatever you have learned in your life, as soon as possible. This will definitely help you change your life positively. Don't rush through these things. Take your time and implement these things slowly.

Thank you and good luck.

About the Author

Hi, I'm **Mark** and here's a little about me:

I'm an entrepreneur, internet marketer, author, life coach, professional speaker, fitness enthusiast, and world traveler. I feel extremely blessed for the life that I live.

I bring 7 years of niche expertise in self-help and personal development. I'm a business management graduate and I like to study people who appear to be unbeatable against all oddities or challenges of life. I seek answers for failures, lack of growth and thus I want to help people reinvent themselves. I believe: Each and every person is the sole controller of his/her life. If you do not take an utmost care of your life, no one else will.

One Last Thing...

If you enjoyed this book or found it useful I'd be very grateful if you'd post a short review on Amazon. Your support really does make a difference and I read all the reviews personally so I can get your feedback and make this book even better.

Thanks again for your support!

www.ingramcontent.com/pod-product-compliance
Lightning Source LLC
Chambersburg PA
CBHW061930280526
45787CB00004B/1549